Carlo Cestra

The Itali
Heavy Cruiser
Pola

KAGERO

The Italian Heavy Cruiser *Pola*, 1941
– the port side view.

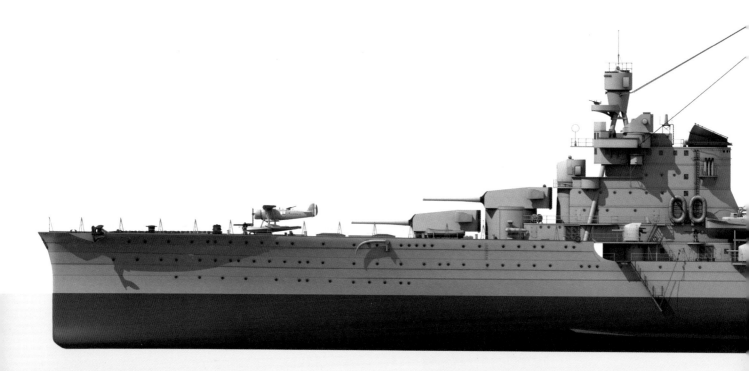

Overview

The *Pola* was a Zara-class heavy cruiser of the Italian Regia Marina operating during the Second World War. She was the last of four ships in this class (*Zara, Fiume e Gorizia* were the other three), built in the Odero Terni Orlando shipyard in Livorno in 1930 she entered service in 1932.

At the beginning of 1928, the Italian Regia Marina, not to be disadvantaged compared to the other navies, needed to build new cruisers whose could be used with the Trento-class ships, while waiting until the economic resources of the Italian state allowed it to get new battleships or to renovate old ones like *Cavour* or *Giulio Cesare*.

Since there was a halt in building and the study of projects, the only existing one was what the Navy Ministry had prepared was for a Trento-class cruiser in which the thickness of the armour was increased to 150 mm.

In fact, it was necessary to produce other cruisers more resistant to combat to the lighter ones, too vulnerable to constitute the core of the support units.

Keeping unchanged the armament and reducing slightly the speed it seemed possible that the vessels can be built without exceeding the standard displacement of 10,000 tons set by the Treaty of Washington.

Anyway the instructions for the study of these cuisers were not to determined from the beginning the displacement and not to be tie up to the limit imposed in Washington for the heavy cruisers.

It was also important that the new heavy cruisers had extensive vertical and horizontal protection, but also a robust hull structure. It was decided to equip them with a main armament of eight 203 mm guns, as on the Trento-class cruisers, and to provide them with an effective operating speed of 32 knots.

To increase the protection of the new cruisers, providing them with a 200 mm armour without exceeding 10,000 tons, it was necessary to reduce the main armament to six 203 guns. This could be possible if there had been the economic resources necessary to order three ships, but at that time, it was hard to obtain it quickly. So the Italian Regia Marina ordered just two cruisers with sixteen guns instead of twelve, with an armament of eight 203 guns and reduced protection of 150 mm of armor.

In 1928 it was decided to build the first two Zara-class cruisers (namely *Zara* and *Fiume*) and later in 1929 the *Gorizia* and finally in 1930 the *Pola*. The building of the *Pola* cost 114 millions and 700.000 liras. *Pola*, at the end of the building, like the other three cruisers of the same class, all entered into service between 1931 and 1932, turned out to be 12,000 tons, although officially reported of 10,000 British tons.

Her motto was "I dare in any undertaking".

Top view.

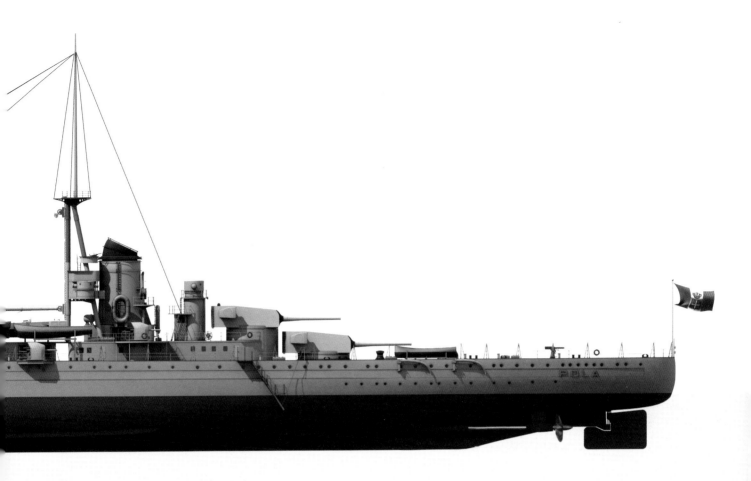

Design, propulsion and armour

Compared to the Trento-class, the Zara-class had a more squat hull, in fact their length was reduced by 14 metres, and it was less suitable for high speed. She had a big bridge structure, that included the fore bridge, the turret and the bow–funnel.

To give them good seakeeping they were equipped with a prow-castle and this solution, compared with the flush-deck of the *Trento*-class, had the advantage of a considerable saving of weight. The bow was straight ahead to the waterline and it had an arched and very flared shape up to the foredeck.

The stern was very rounded and the rudder was semi-compensed and similar to the *Trento* ones.

The hangar for the storage of the two floatplanes was built into the hull structure at the bow of the first 203 turret. An elevator lifted the floatplane on the castle bridge where the "Gagnotto" catapult was placed, which extended to the extreme bow.

The ship was protected with a armoured belt that was 150 mm thick amidships. Her deck armor was 70 mm thick in the central portion of the ship and reduced to 20 mm at either end. The gun turrets had 150 mm thick plating on their faces and the barbettes they sat in were also 150 mm thick. The main superstructure had 150 mm thick sides.

The *Pola* was designed to function as a squadron flagship, so her forward superstructure was larger than that of her sisters, and was faired into the fore funnel.

The vertical protection consisted in a partial belt 150 mm thick at water-line and 100 mm in the lower side part. It continued between the two extreme turrets where it ended with a deck girder 120 mm thick. In height the armored belt reached the protected bridge 70 mm thick. The sides above the belt armor had 30 mm thick to the main deck, that was protected by steel plates 20 mm thick. The turrets and the 203 mm barbettes had 150 mm armor, as was also the armored structure for the direction of the shot. The steering –gear deck of the rudder was protected by a 20 mm bridge.

The engine was made up of eight water-pipe boilers with Thornycroft overheaters. They produced steam to the maximum operating pressure of 25 kg/cm2 with a 60° overheating. The disposition of the boilers was in separated rooms: two at the bow of the prow engine and another one laterally from this; four in the center of the ship between the two groups of engines and another one laterally from the stern group. The boilers fed two "Parsons" steam turbines that fed power to a couple of three blade "Scaglia" screws.

Her engines were rated at 95,000 sh (71,000 kW) and produced a top speed of 32 knots (59 km/h; 37 mph).

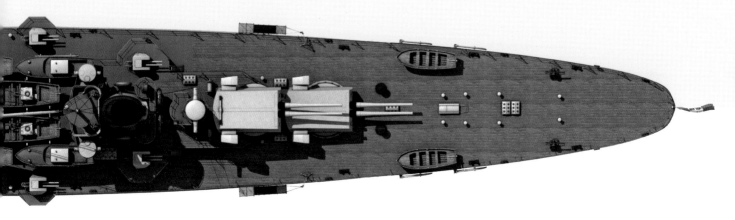

The Italian Heavy Cruiser *Pola*, 1941
– the starboard side.

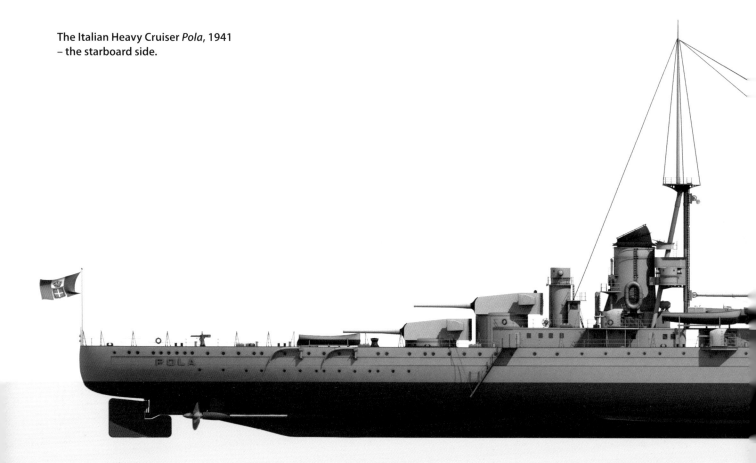

The cruiser was built as a flagship with a larger superstructure to accomodate an admiral's staff.

She had a crew of 31 officers and 810 men.

Armament

The *Pola* was armed with a main battery of eight 203 mm Mod 29 53-caliber guns in four gun turrets. The turrets were arranged in superpositioned pairs forward and aft. Anti-aircraft defense was provided by a battery of sixteen 100 mm 47-cal. guns in twin mounts, four 40 mm guns in single mounts and eight 12.7 mm guns in twin mounts. She carried a pair of IMAM Ro.43 floatplanes for aerial reconnaissance; the hangar was located under the forecastle and a fixed catapult was mounted on the centerline at the bow. *Pola*'s secondary armament was revised several times during her career. Two of the 100 mm guns and all of the 40 mm and 12.7 mm guns were removed in the late 1930s, eight 37 mm 54-cal. guns and eight 13.2 mm guns were installed in their place. Two 120 mm 15-cal. starshell guns were added in 1940.

Service

The *Pola* entered service on 21 December 1932 and participated in a naval review in the Gulf of Naples and she hosted Benito Mussoilini on 6-7 july 1933. In the first years she served in coastal region and in the Mediterranean. On 29 July 1934 she was formally given her battle flag in a ceremony in her namesake city.

Between 1936 and 1937 she was engaged in the operations of the Spanish Civil War. On 3 September 1936 she left Gaeta, bound for spanish waters. She began in the First Division of the First Team as a non-intervention patrol and from 10 September to 3 October 1936 she was stationed in Palma de Mallorca to safeguard Italian interests there.

On 10-12 March 1937 she went to Italian Libya with Mussolini and Prince Luigi Amedeo aboard.

On 7 June 1937 she took part in a naval review in the Gulf of Naples held for the visiting German Field Marshal Weerner von Blomberg.

On 5 May 1938 another review took place when Adolf Hitler made a visit to Italy.

On 7 March 1939 the four *Zara* class cruisers sortied from Taranto to intercept a squadron of Republican warships, three cruisers and eight destroyers, attempting to reach the Black Sea. The Italian cruisers were ordered not to open fire but trying to impede the progress of the Spanish ships and to force them to dock at Augusta in Sicily. The Spanish commander refused and steamed to French Tunisia, where the ships were interned.

On 7-9 April 1939 the *Pola* provided gunfire support to Italian forces occupying Albania.

On 10 June 1940 *Pola* became the flagship of the 2nd Squadron, which also included the three *Trento*-class cruisers, three light cruisers of the Seventh Division, and seventeen destroyers, so she was assigned to Admiral Riccardo Paladini.

On 6 July 1940 *Pola* and the remainder of the 2nd Squadron escorted a convoy bound to North Africa; on the 7th Italian reconnaissance reported a British cruiser squadron to have arrived in Malta so the Italian naval high command therefore ordered several other cruisers and destroyers from the 1st Squadron to join the escort for the convoy. The battleships *Conte di Cavour* and *Giulio Cesare* provided distant support. On 9 July 1940 *Pola* took part in the battle of Punta Stilo, opening fire against British aircraft and ships.

From 30 of July to 1 of August 1940 was part of the indirect escort, with the *Trento* and the *Gorizia* to a couple of convoys going to Tripoli and Bengasi, with other cruisers of the First, Fourth and Seventh Divisions. At the end of August she was transferred from Naples to Taranto where, in the night of 11 and 12 November 1940, the British fleet launched the night-time carrier strike in the harbor, but she was not attacked in the raid. *Pola* and the rest of the fleet left for Naples the following morning.

The Italian fleet left the harbor on 26 November 1940 and, while en route to the British fleet, *Pola* and the battleship *Vittorio Veneto* were attacked by Swordfish Torpedo bombers from the carrier *HMS*

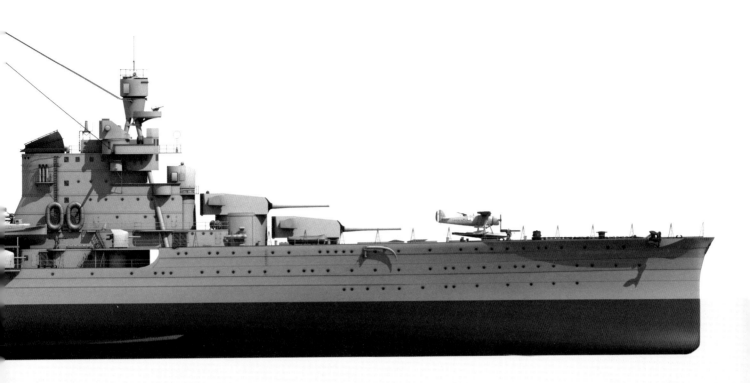

Ark Royal, but both ships evaded the torpedoes. On 27th she took part in Capo Teulada, also named the battle of Capo Spartivento: the two fleets then clashed in an engagement that lasted for about an hour and Pola fired 118 shots of 203 mm against the British cruiser HMS Berwick disabling one of her main gun turrets. In spite of this, Admiral Inigo Campioni broke off the action because he mistakenly believed he was facing a superior force, the result of poor aerial reconnaissance.

The Italian fleet was reorganized on 9 December, and the Pola joined her three sister ships in the 3rd Division of the 1st Squadron, which was now commanded by Admiral Angelo Iachino.

On 14 December 1940 the Pola was seriously hit during a British night attack in the port of Naples. Two bombs hit the ship, both amidships on the port side. The hits damaged three of the ship's boilers and caused significant flooding and a significant list to port.

On 16 December the ship was placed in dock until 7 February 1941.

She returned to Taranto on 13 February to join Zara and Fiume for extensive maneuvers and night-time traning operations off Taranto that took place from 11 to 24 March 1941.

The sinking

During the Second World War the Zara class cruisers couldn't demonstrate all of their operational possibilities because the Matapan Battle, on the south west coast of the Peloponnesian peninsula of Greece, entirely destroyed the Division.

In late March 1941 the British ships of the Mediterranean Fleet covered troop movements to Greece. At Bletchley Park the British cryptographers read a message that reporting the sailing of an Italian battle fleet comprising one battleship (Vittorio Veneto), six heavy cruisers (among them Pola) and two light cruisers plus destroyers, to attack the merchant convoy supplying the British forces, at the south of island of Crete.

At the same time the Italians had been wrongly informed that the Mediterranean Fleet had only one operational battleship and no aircraft carrier. In reality there were three battleships (HMS Barham, Valiant and Warspite), two Flotillas of destroyers (among them, in the 14th Flotilla,

General characteristics

Name:	Pola
Class and type:	*Zara*-class cruisers
Displacement:	13,531 tons - Full load 14.360 tons
Barehull:	2,987 tons
Protection:	2,681 tons
Fitting out:	1,513 tons
Engine apparatus:	1,409 tons
Army equipment:	1,328 tons
Movable weights, complementaries and various	858 tons
Length:	182.8 m (599.9 ft)
Beam:	20.6 m (67.7 ft)
Draft:	7.2 m (23.7 ft)
Engines:	8 Thornycroft boilers
Power:	95.000 SHP (71.000 kW)
Propulsion:	2 groups of "Parsons" steam turbines, 2 propellers
Speed:	32 knots (59 km/h; 37 mph)
Range:	5,230 miles at 16 knots
	3,310 miles at 25 knots
	1,915 miles at 31,5 knots
Fuel:	1,540 tons (up to 2320 tons)
Armament:	8 x 203/53 mm cal guns
	16 x 100/47 mm OTO Mod. 1927 anti-aircraft cal guns
	6 x 40/39 mm Vickers_Terni guns
	4 x 2 13,2 mm Breda Mod. 31 guns
	1 fixed catapult
Armor:	Main belt: 150 mm
	Deck: 70 mm
	Large-caliber turrets: 150 mm
	Superstructure: 150 mm
Aircraft carried:	2 floatplanes IMAM Ro.43
Crew:	31 officers and 810 men

there were HMS Jervis and Nubian), Australian and British light cruisers, and the damaged British aircraft carrier HMS Illustrious had been replaced by HMS Formidable.

The Italian fleet was led by Iachino's flagship, the battleship Vittorio Veneto, and included the entire heavy cruiser force (Zara, Fiume, Pola, Trieste, Trento e Bolzano), thirteen destroyers and two light cruisers (Duca degli Abruzzi and Giuseppe Garibaldi).

None of the Italian ships had radar, while the Allied ships did.

On 27 March Vice Admiral Pridham-Wippel, with four cruisers and a number of destroyers, sailed from Greece for a position to the south of Crete. On the same time Admiral Cunningham with the *Formidable, Warspite, Barham* and *Valiant* left Alexandria to meet the cruisers.

The Italian Fleet was spotted by a British Sunderland Flying boat depriving it of any advantage of surprise. Admiral Iachino also knew about the *Formidable* thanks to the decryption team aboard *Vittorio Veneto*, but the Italian headquarters decided, wrongly, to go ahead with the operation, to show their fighting ability and their confidence in the higher speed of their warships.

On 28 March, early in the morning, an Imam Ro.43 floatplane launched by *Vittorio Veneto* spotted the British cruiser squadron, while the *Trento* group encountered the British cruiser group south of the Greek island of Gavdos. *Trieste, Trento* and *Bolzano* fired repeatedly, thinking to hit them, but after an hour, as the distance had not been reduced, the Italian cruisers broke off the chase and returned to the north west to rejoin the *Vittorio Veneto*. The allied ships followed the Italian cruisers at extreme range and Admiral Iachino let them come on, in hopes of luring the British cruisers into the range of *Vittorio Veneto*'s guns. When the Allied reached the Italian cruisers, *Vittorio Veneto* opened fire on the British ships but she was too far and they suffered only slight damage.

During the same day Cunningham's force attacked the Italian fleet three times, also with torpedo bombers and they damaged *Vittorio Veneto*. During the night, Admiral Iachino deployed his ships in three columns and used smoke, searchlights and a heavy barrage to protect his battleship. This tactic protected the *Vittorio Veneto*, but one torpedo, launched from an allied aircraft, hit the *Pola*, which had nearly stopped to avoid running into the *Fiume* and could not take any avoiding action. This hit knocked out five boilers and the main steam line, causing *Pola* to lose electric power and drift to a stop.

She was stopped and isolated.

The squadron did not start to return towards her until about an hour later, after the order had been given by Iachino, officially due to communication problems, while *Vittorio Veneto* and the other ships continued to Taranto. When the other two cruisers of the First Division, *Zara* and *Fiume*, went to help her, the bulk of the Allied forces detected the Italian squadron on radar and they were able to close without being detected. The Italian ships had no radar and could not detect British ships by any means other than sight. The Italians had their main gun batteries disarmed. The Allied searchlights from *Valiant* illuminated their enemy. Some British gunners witnessed the cruiser's main turrets flying dozens of metres into the air. After just three minutes, *Fiume* and *Zara* had been destroyed. *Fiume* sank and *Zara* was finished off by a torpedo from the destroyer *HMS Jervis* during the night of 29 March.

Pola watched powerless the end of her division units and her captain, assuming that his ship would be the next target, ordered his crew to open the seacocks and to abandon ship.

Two Italian destroyers were sunk in the first five minutes. The other two managed to escape, the former with heavy damage. The only known Italian reaction after the shocking surprise was a fruitless torpedo attack by some destroyers and the ineffective fire of one of *Zara*'s 40 mm guns in the direction of the British warships.

The radar of the British destroyer *Havock* descovered *Pola* six miles to port, apparently dead in the water, without power and in darkness: she was already sinking. Towing her to Alexandria as a prize was

Back view.

considered, but daylight was approaching and it was thought that the danger of enemy air attack was too high.

The British destroyer HMS *Jervis*, 14th Flotilla, approached her: they saw that most of her crew had jumped into the water, and the remaining men were huddled on the forecastle, ready to surrender. *Jervis* stood by and recovered the surviving 22 officers and 236 enlisted men from *Pola*.

Soon after two torpedoes had been fired by *Jervis* and one by *Nubian*, speeded up the sinking of *Pola*.

Admiral Cunningham ordered a signal to be made on the Merchant Marine emergency band. This signal was received by the Italian High Command. It informed them that, due to air strikes, the Allied ships had ceased their rescue operations and they granted safe passage to a hospital ship for rescue purposes. The location of the remaining survivors was broadcast and the Italian hospital ship *Gradisca* came to recover them.

Matapan was Italy's greatest defeat at sea removing from its order of battle a cruiser division, because the Regia Marina had lost three in one night. That the Italians had sortied so far to the east established a potential threat that forced the British to keep their battleships ready to face another sortie during the operations off Greece and Crete.

After the defeat at Cape Matapan, the Italian Admiral Iachino wrote that the battle had "the consequence of limiting our operational activities for some time, not for the serious moral effect of the losses, as the British believed, but because the operation revealed our inferiority in effective aero-naval cooperation and the backwardness of our night battle technology."

The *Pola* has perished south of Capo Matapan at position 35°15' North latitude and 21° East longitude. A total of 328 men went down with the ship.

Pola was formally stricken from the naval register on 18 October 1946.

Conclusion

These *Zara*-class cruisers were for that time, and for the Italian technical and economic possibilities, excellent combat vessels. The main concept was that, not having the quantitative supiriority, was necessary to improve their quality by the development of the ability capable of prevailing on the battlefield.

In the period of her service (9 years service life) *Pola* made twelve missions, including eight in search of the enemy, three for escort and convoy protection and one for protection of vessels appointed to place a minefield. She covered 13.174 mi (21.200 km) in wartime sailing, using 8.813 tons of fuel oil in 611 hours of navigation. She was inactive for 57 days.

The *Zara* cruisers at that time represented original creations that inspired foreign constructions and they helped to rectify a great mistake, typical of the "Washington" cruisers, of high speed as the main feature to the detriment of their protection.

Carreer

Ordered:	1930
Shipyard:	Cantiere Odero Terni Orlando - Livorno
Laid down:	17 March 1931
Launched:	5 December 1931
Commissioned:	21 December 1932
Fate:	Sunk 29 March 1941

Bibliography

"Gli Incrociatori Italiani (The Italian Cruisers)" – Ufficio Storico della Marina Militare Italiana

View of the ship's hull and
superstructure from the port side.

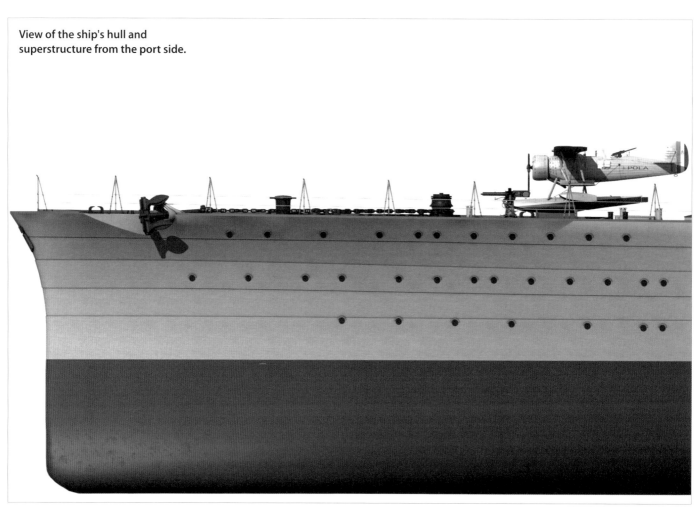

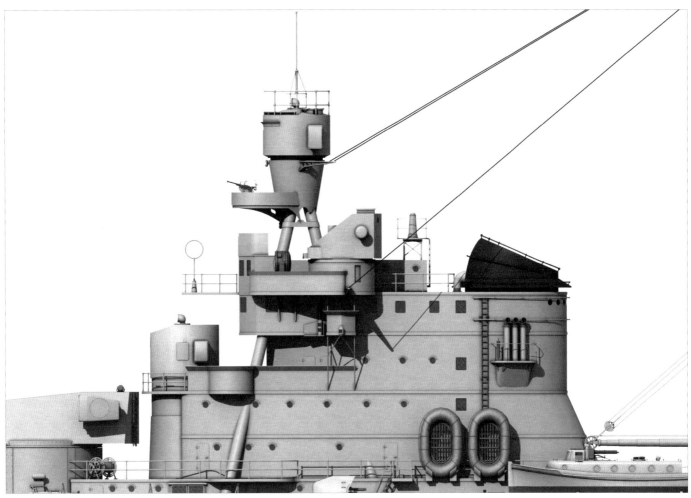

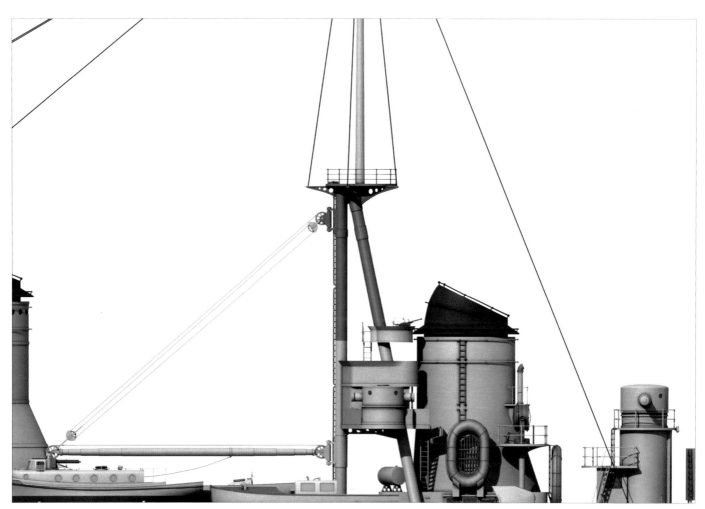

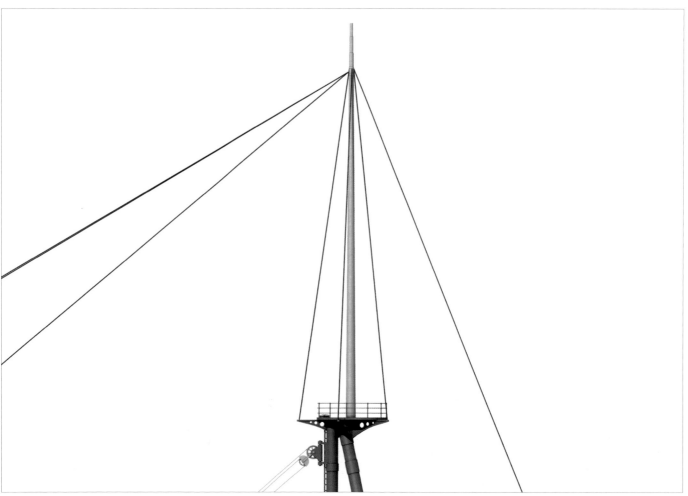

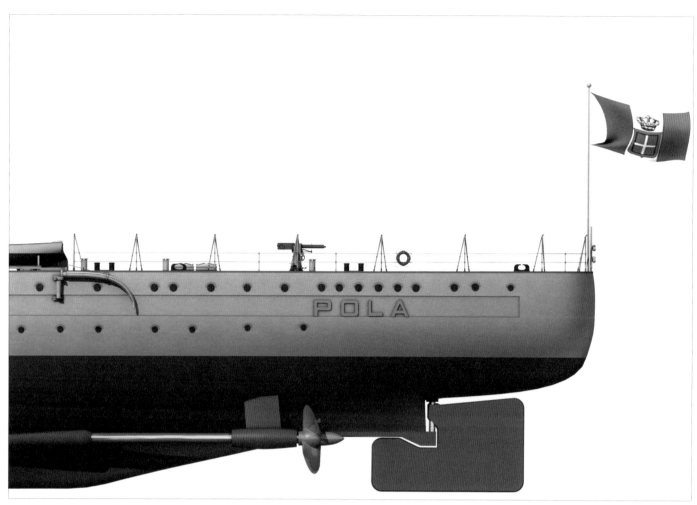

View of the ship's hull and superstructure
from the starboard side.

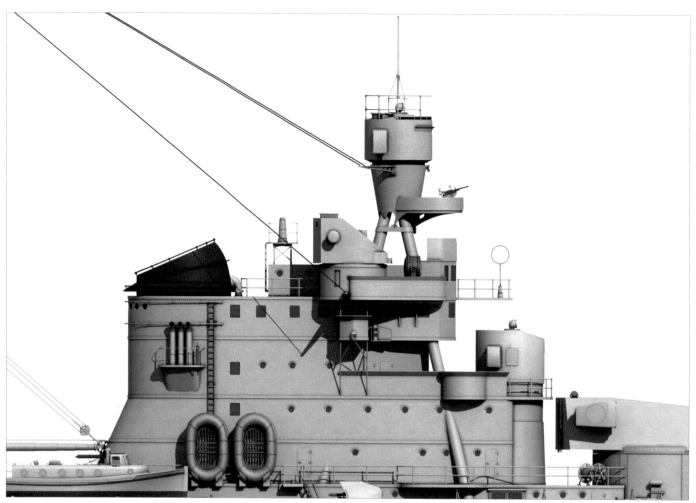

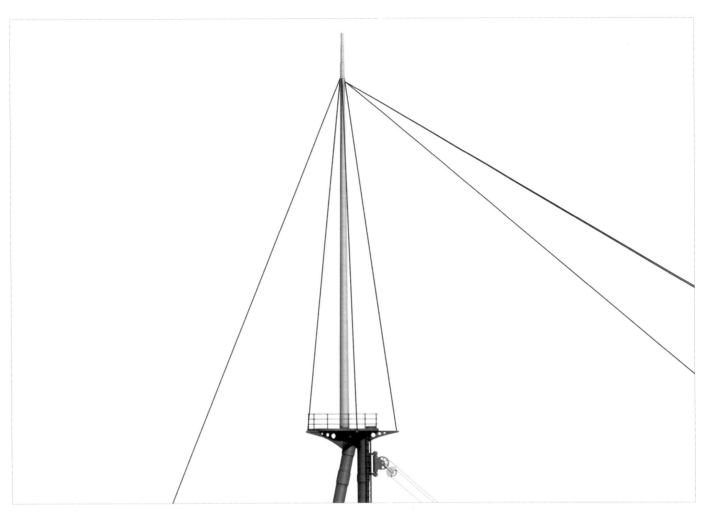

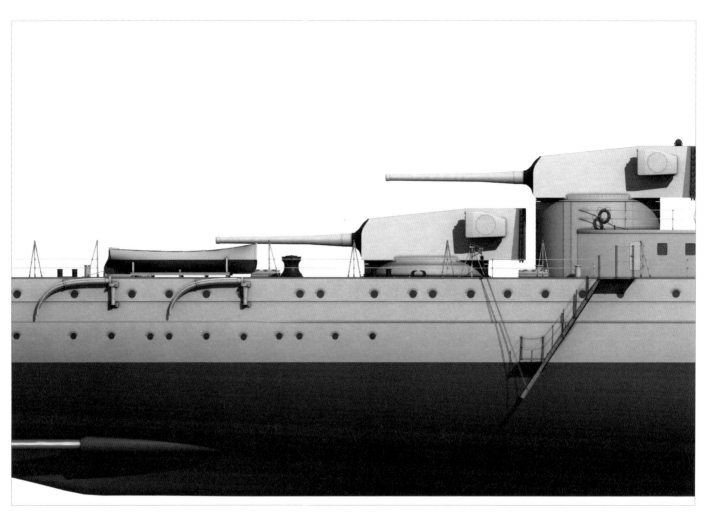

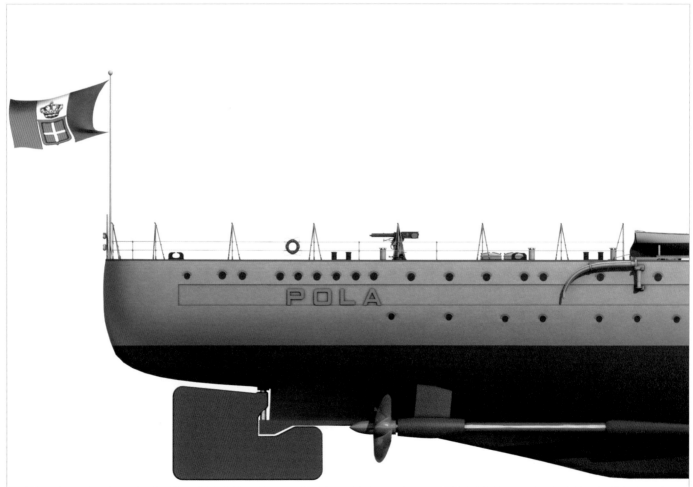

View of the ship's hull and superstructure from above.

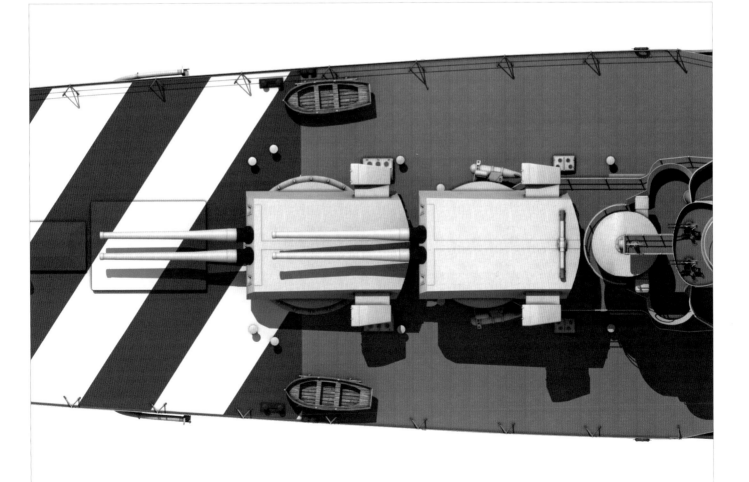

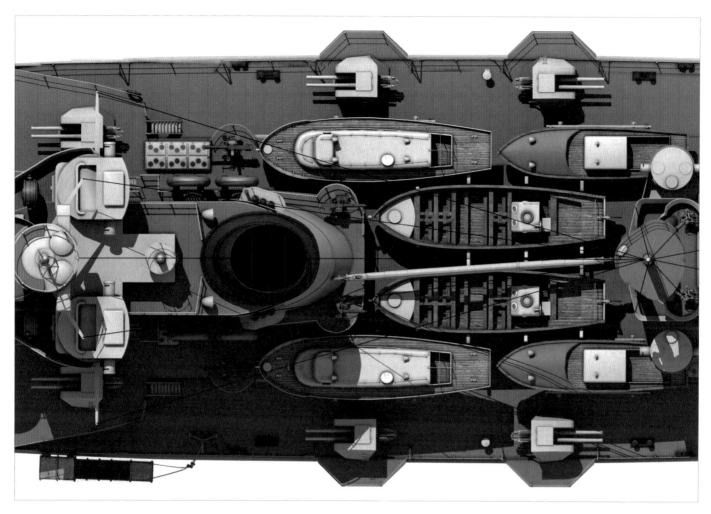

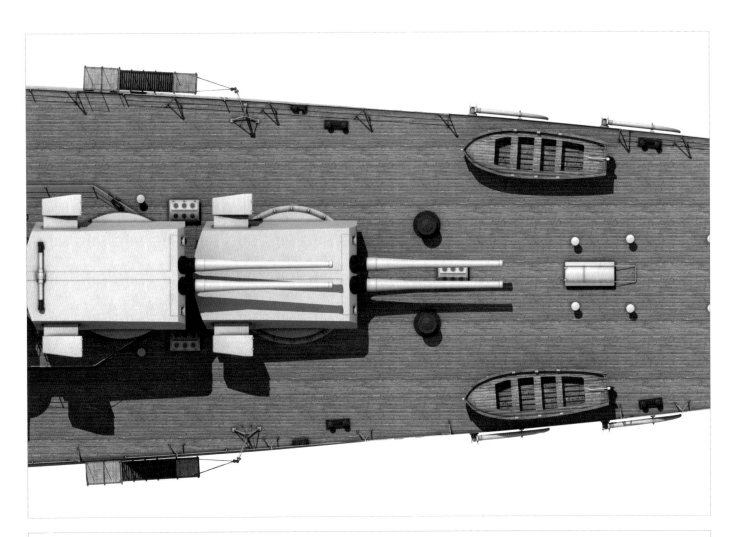

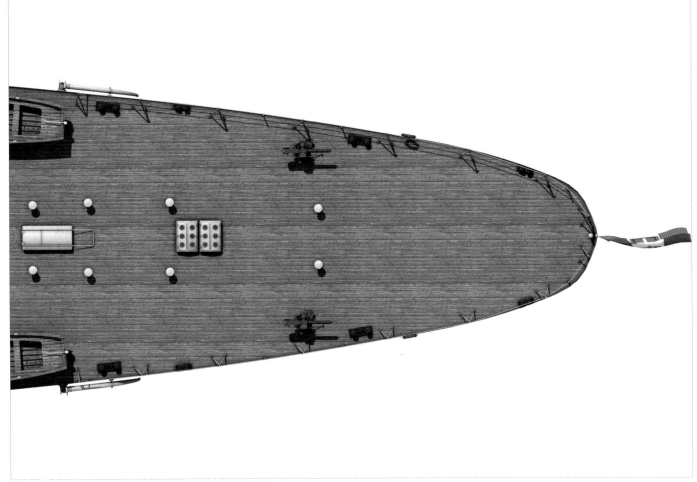

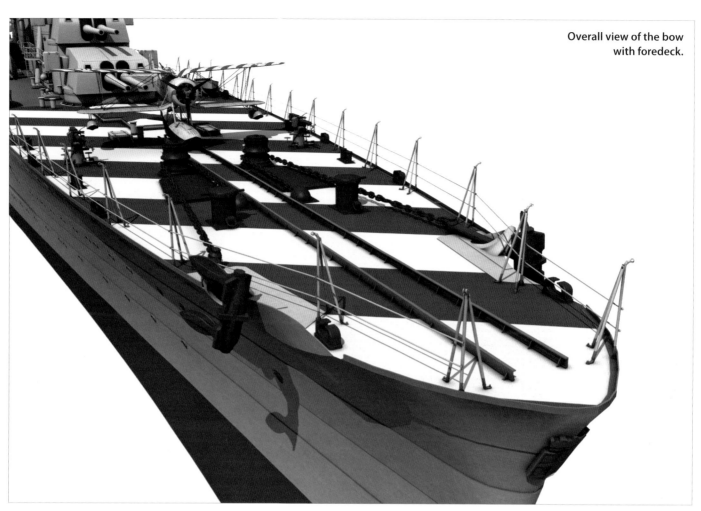

Overall view of the bow with foredeck.

The starboard anchor.

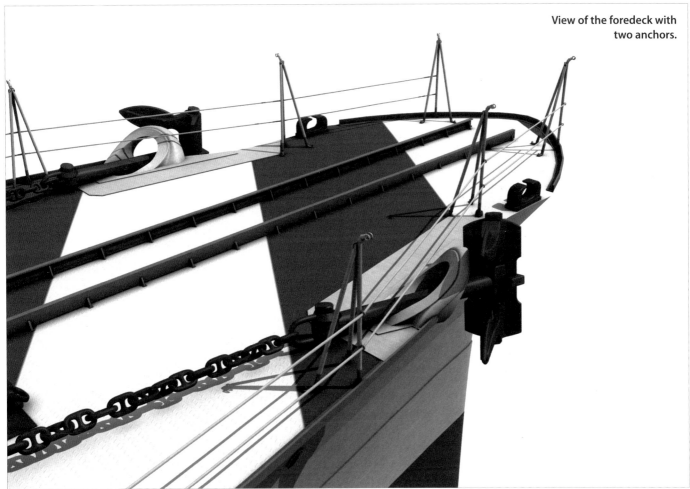

View of the foredeck with
two anchors.

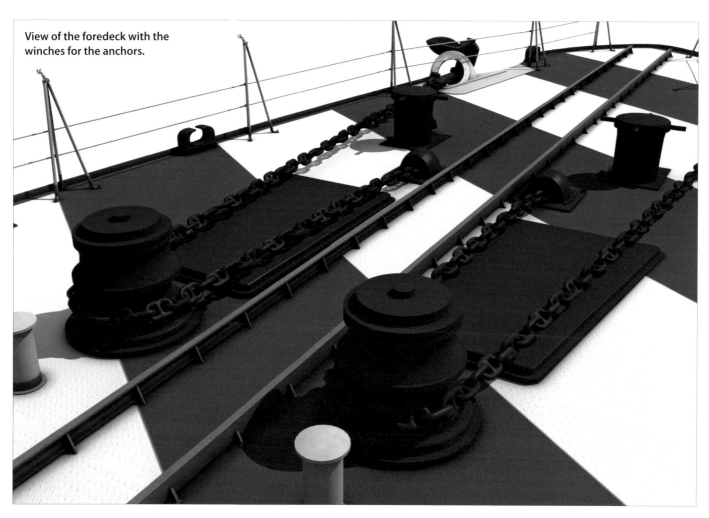

View of the foredeck with the
winches for the anchors.

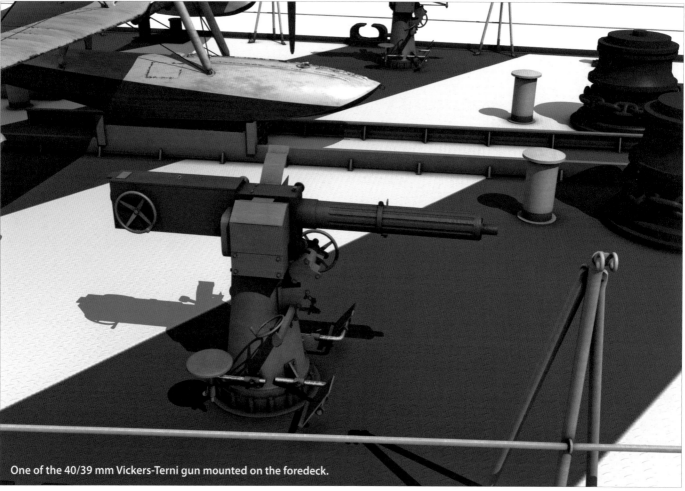

One of the 40/39 mm Vickers-Terni gun mounted on the foredeck.

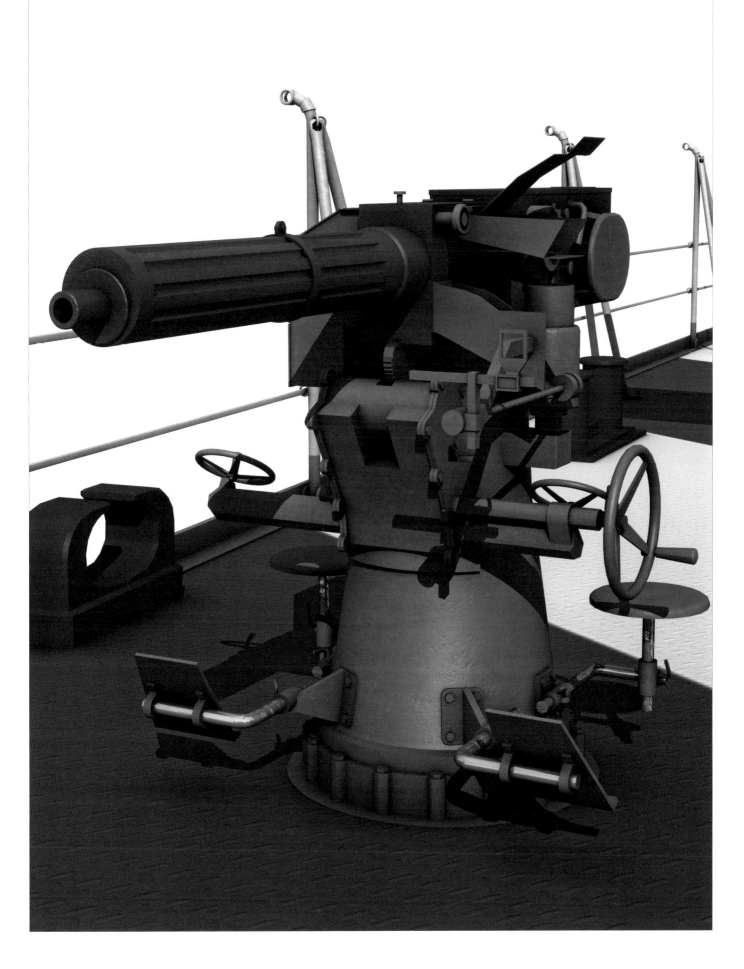

View of a 40/39 mm Vickers-Terni anti-aircraft gun.

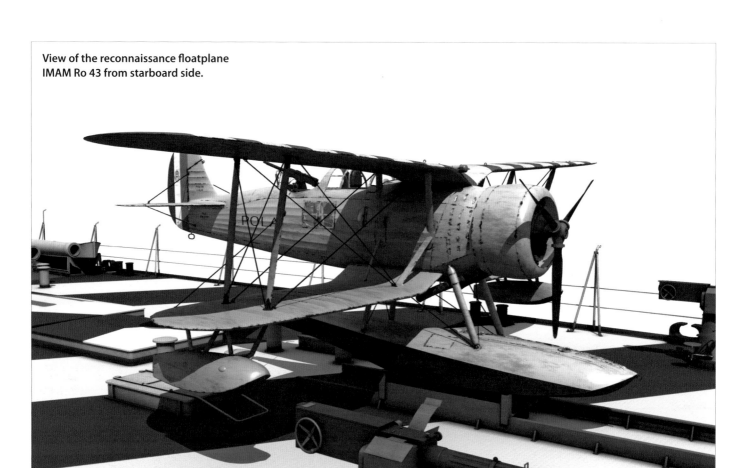

View of the reconnaissance floatplane
IMAM Ro 43 from starboard side.

Overall view of the 203/53 mm
turrets no. 1 and 2.

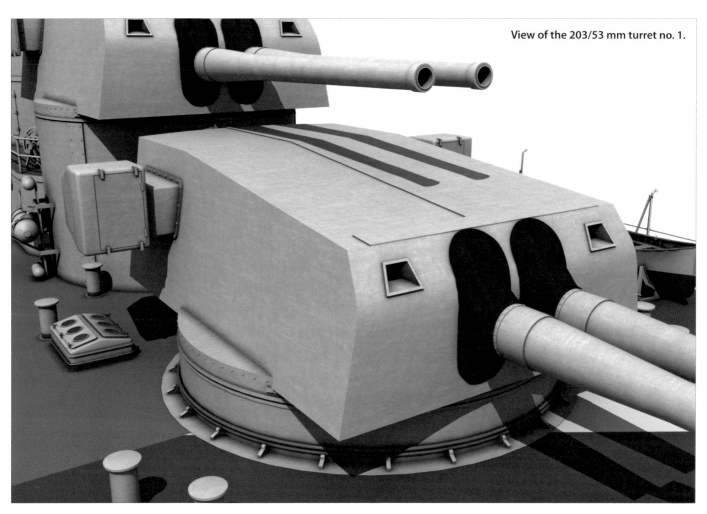

View of the 203/53 mm turret no. 1.

Close-up view of the range finder
of the 203/53 mm turret no. 1.

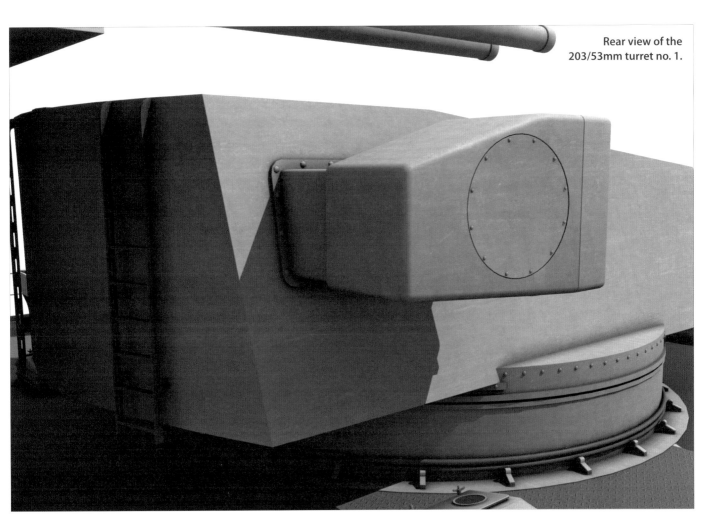

Rear view of the
203/53mm turret no. 1.

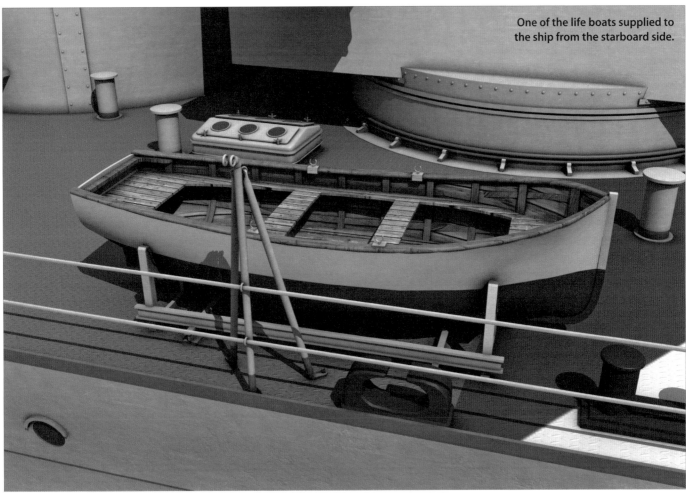

One of the life boats supplied to
the ship from the starboard side.

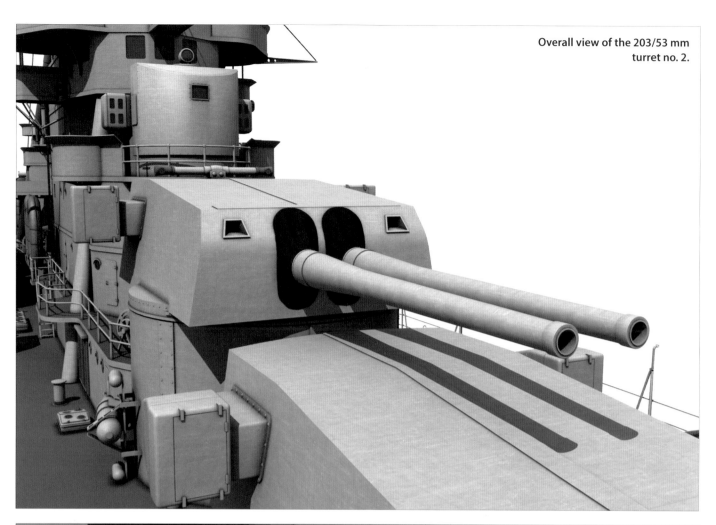

Overall view of the 203/53 mm turret no. 2.

One of the paravanes placed on the sides of the barbette of the 203/53 mm turret no. 2.

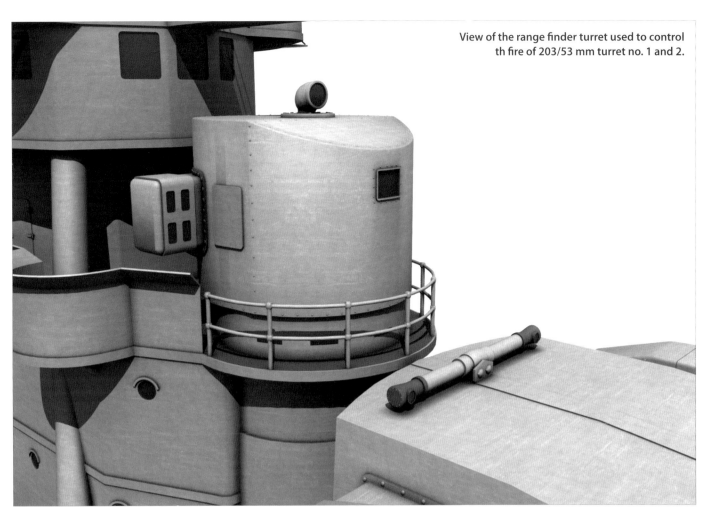

View of the range finder turret used to control
th fire of 203/53 mm turret no. 1 and 2.

Overall view of the aft part of the ship from the starboard side.

Overall view of the superstructure.

Close-up of the superstructure with the green position lights.

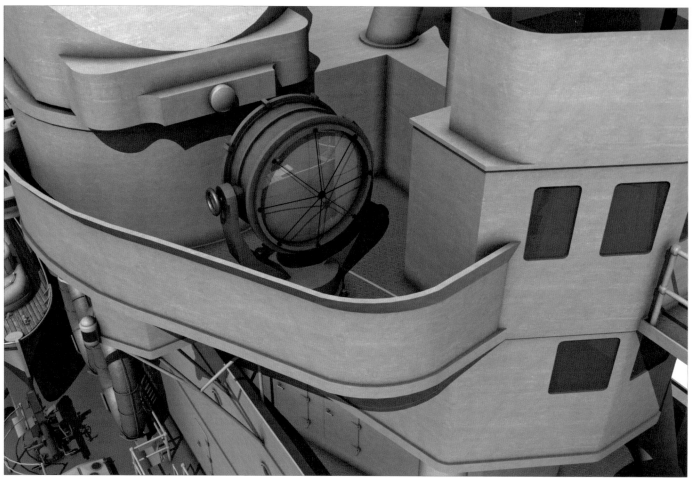

One of the searchlights placed on the superstructure from starboard side.

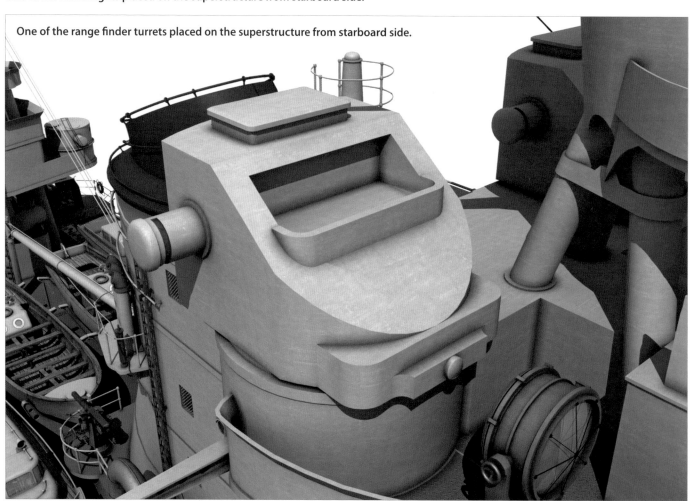

One of the range finder turrets placed on the superstructure from starboard side.

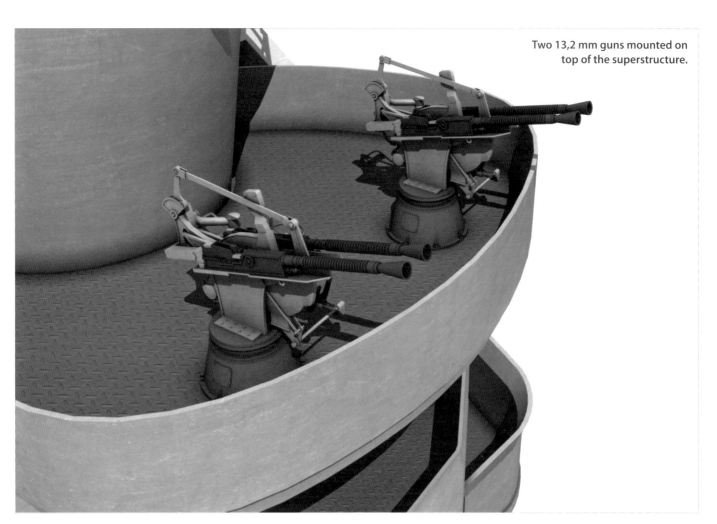

Two 13,2 mm guns mounted on top of the superstructure.

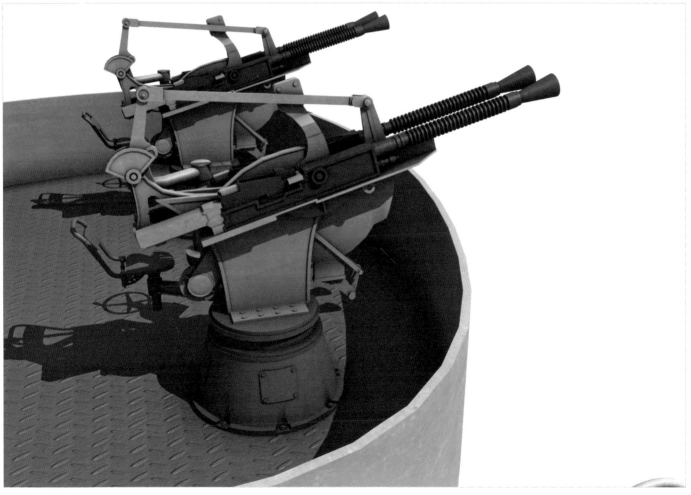

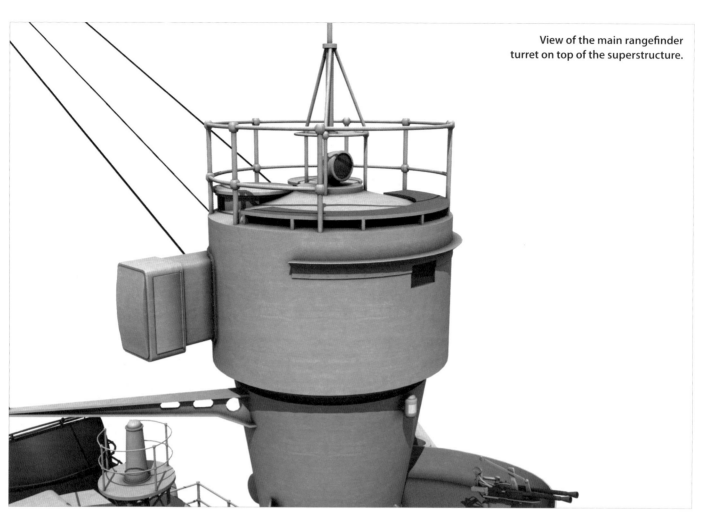

View of the main rangefinder turret on top of the superstructure.

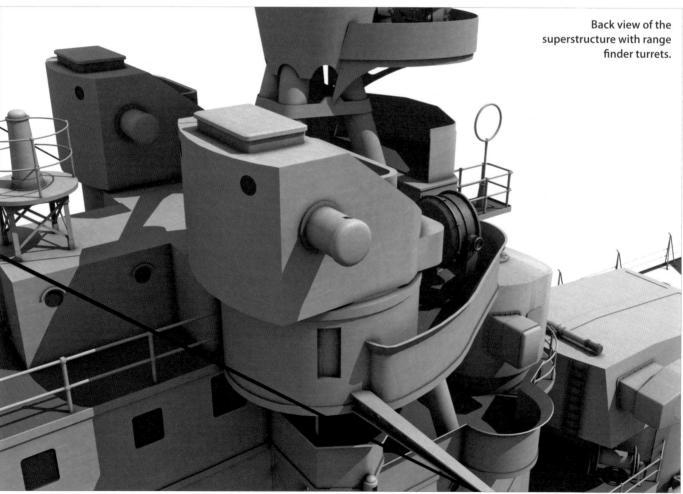

Back view of the superstructure with range finder turrets.

Back view of the superstructure with range finder turrets.

Back view of the 203/53 mm turret no. 2.

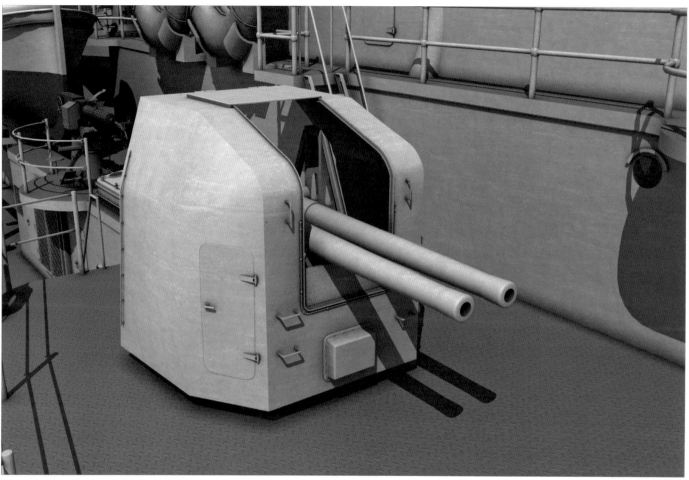
View of a 100/47 mm OTO turret from the starboard side.

View of two life rafts mounted on the superstructure from the starboard side.

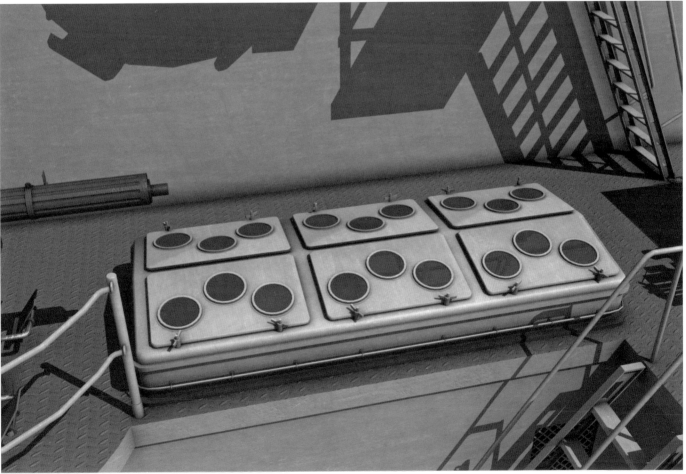

Superstructures on the deck.

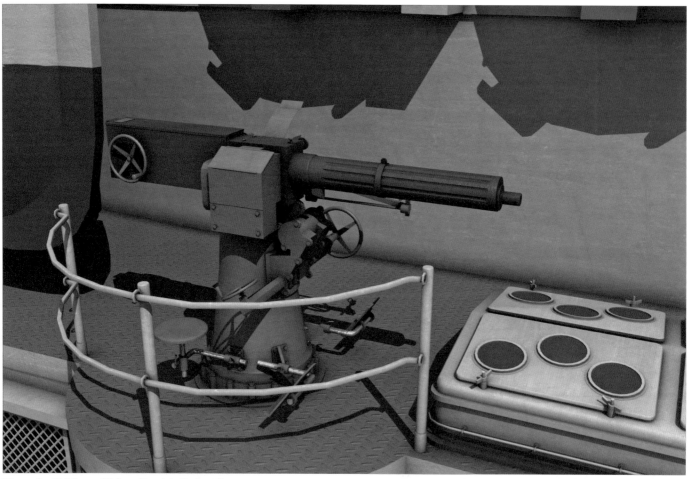

View of a 40/39 mm Vickers-Terni anti-aircraft gun.

View of two 100/47 mm OTO anti-aircraft turrets amidships from starboard side.

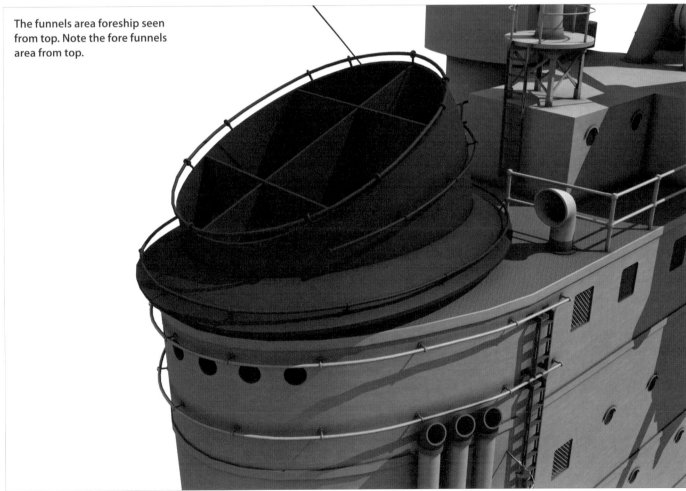

The funnels area foreship seen from top. Note the fore funnels area from top.

View of the fore funnel.

The fore funnel area foreship seen from top. Note the nozzles to emit the smoke screens.

Views of the area with the motor boats from starboard side.

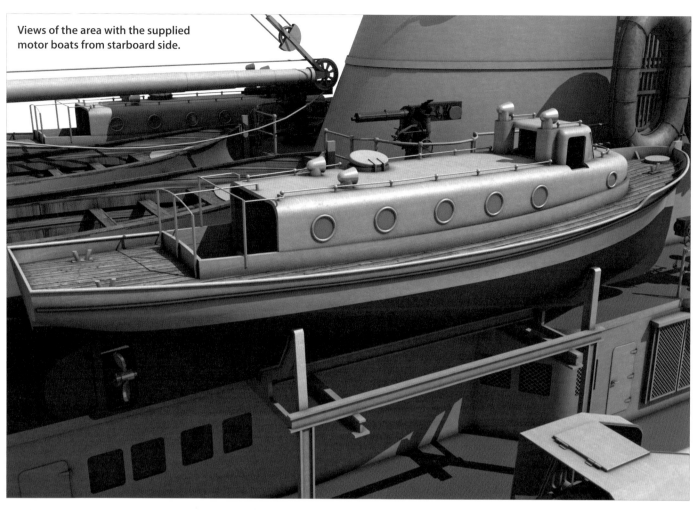

Views of the area with the supplied motor boats from starboard side.

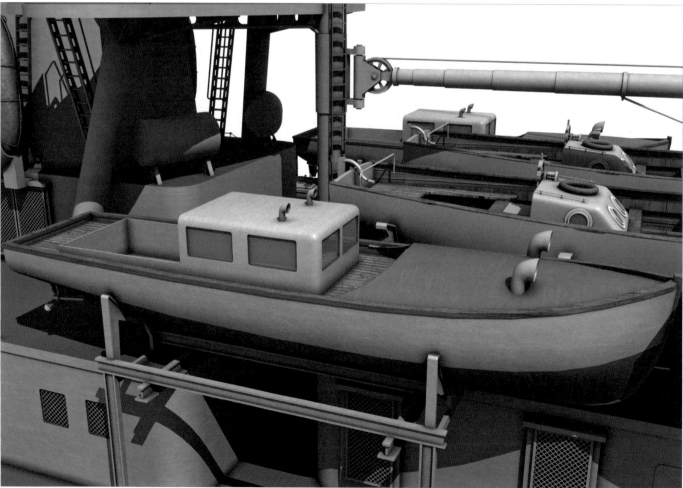

View of a 40/39 mm Vickers-Terni anti-aircraft gun amidships from starboard side.

View of a 100/47 mm OTO turret aft from starboard side.

View of a 100/47 mm OTO turret aft from starboard side.

View of the range finder turret to control the fire of the 100/47 mm turret aft from starboard side.

View of the telemetric turret to control fire of the 100/47 mm turret aft from starboard side.

View of a 13,2 mm guns mounted on the main mast from starboard side.

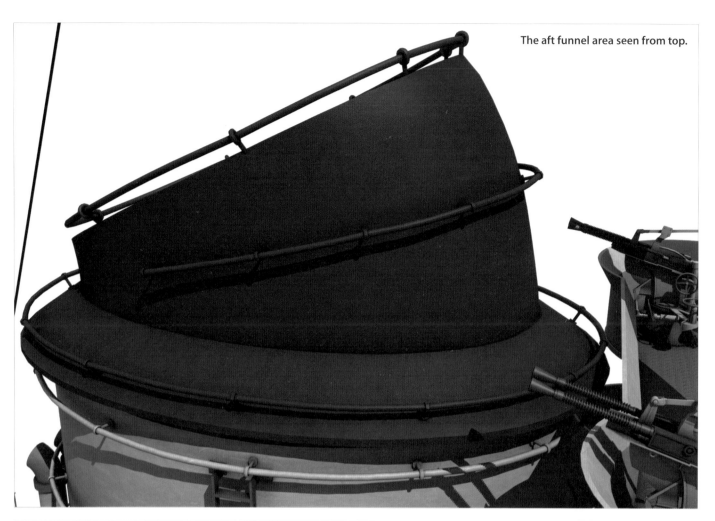

View of the aft funnel.

Close-up view of the searchlights aft from starboard side.

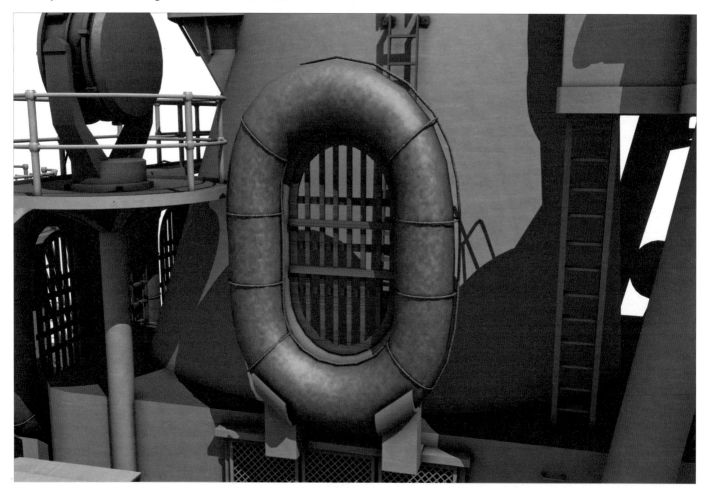

One of the life rafts placed on the side of the funnel aft from starboard side.

View of the structures on the main mast. Note the ladder to reach the crow's nest.

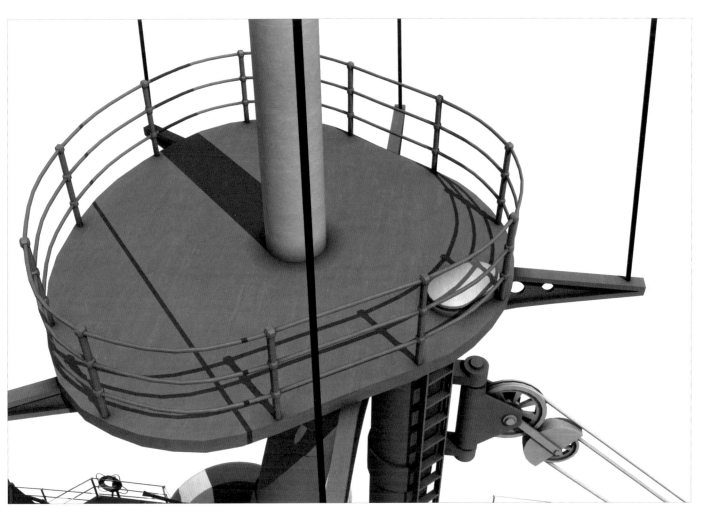

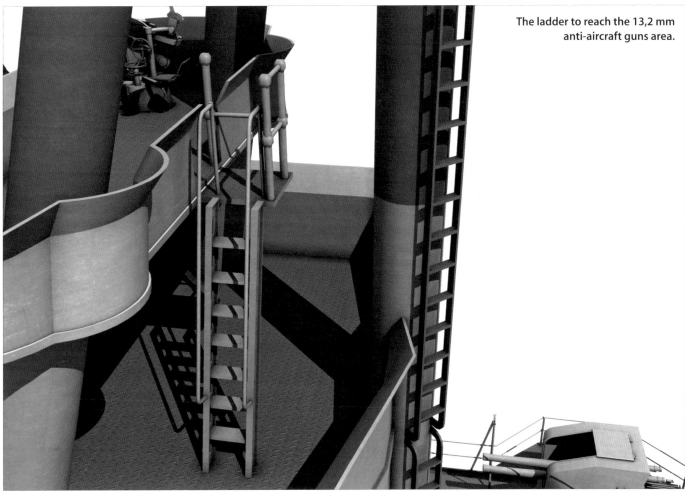

The ladder to reach the 13,2 mm
anti-aircraft guns area.

View of the 100/47 mm OTO turret aft area from starboard side.

View of the range
finder turret to control
fire of the 203/53 mm
turrets no. 3 and 4.

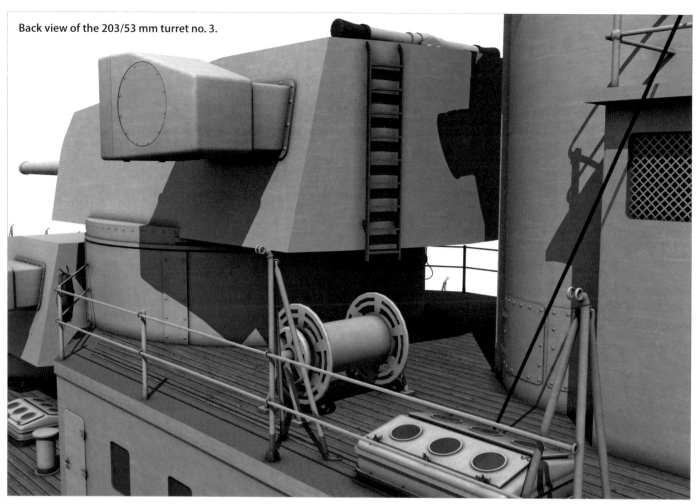

Back view of the 203/53 mm turret no. 3.

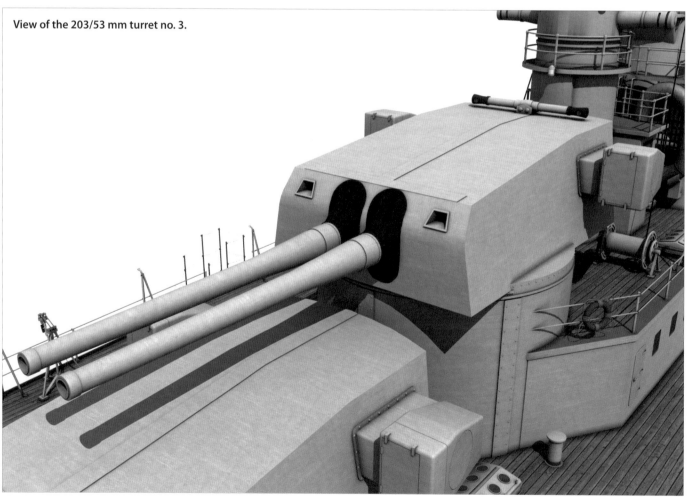

View of the 203/53 mm turret no. 3.

Close-up view of the 203/53 mm turret no. 3.

Rear view of the 203/53 mm turret no. 4.

Overall view of the 203/53 mm
turret no. 4 area.

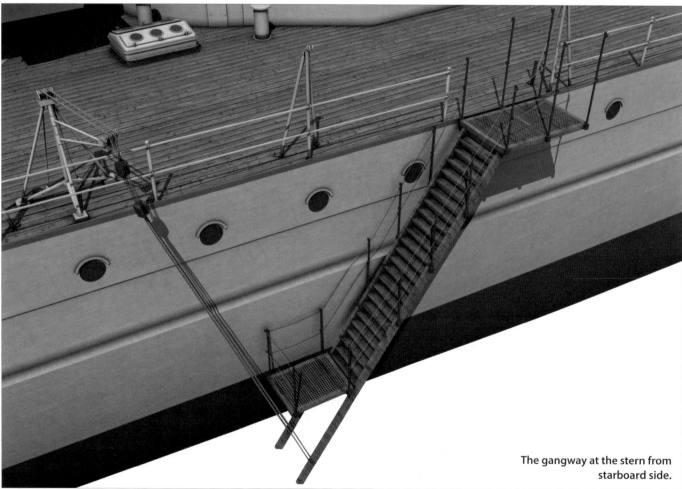

The gangway at the stern from
starboard side.

The gangway at the stern from starboard side.

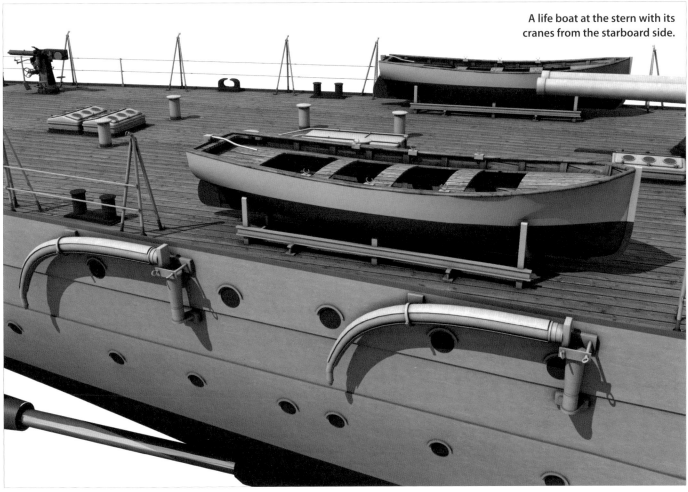

A life boat at the stern with its cranes from the starboard side.

Superstructures on the deck on the stern.

View of a 40/39 mm Vickers-Terni anti-aircraft gun mounted on the stern.

The rudder and propellers area with the ship name on the hull from starboard side.

View of
the stern.

The ship's name from port side.

The 40/39 mm Vickers-Terni anti-aircraft gun mounted on the stern from port side.

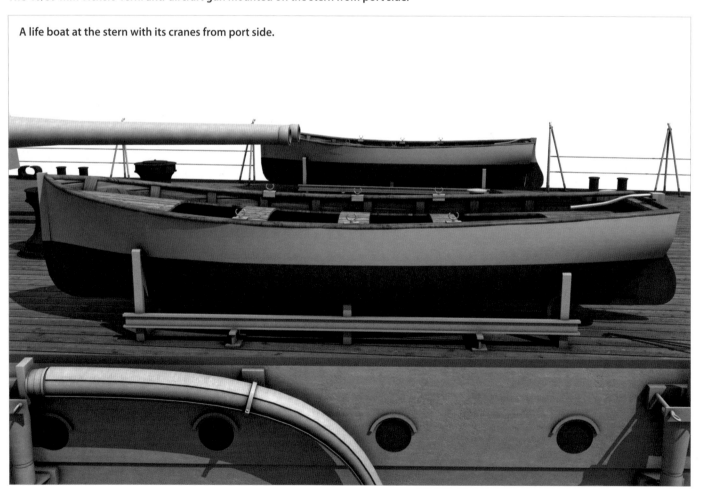

A life boat at the stern with its cranes from port side.

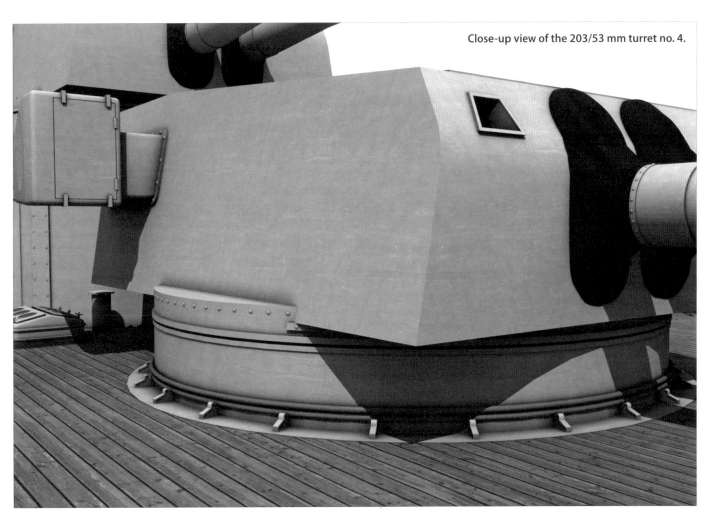

Close-up view of the 203/53 mm turret no. 4.

View of the wooden deck from wooden deck.

Overall view of the
203/53 mm turret no. 3.

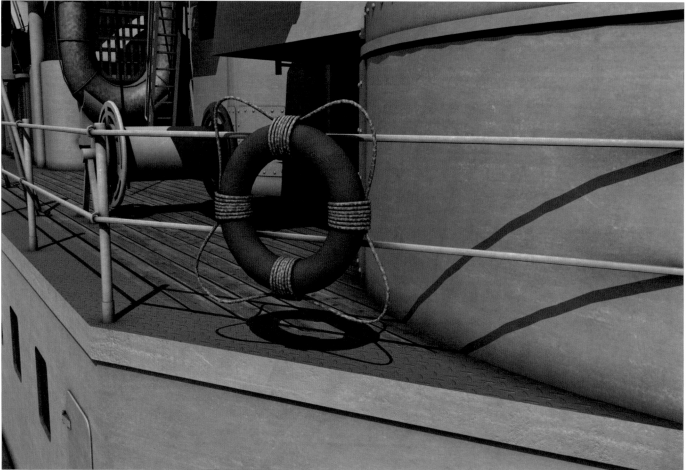

One of the lifebelts.

View of a ladder.

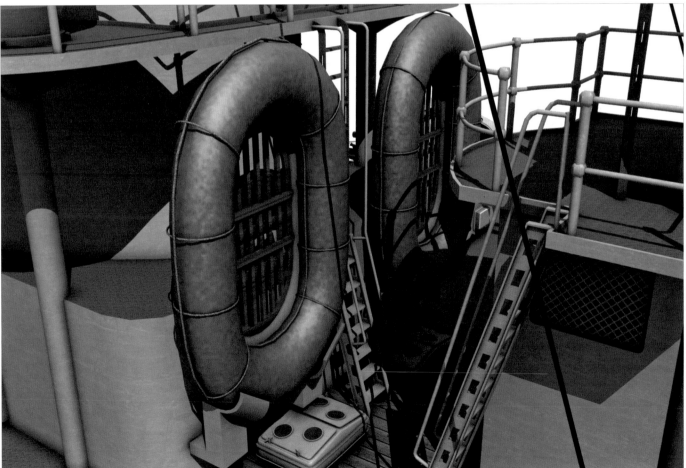

Life rafts placed on the back of the funnel aft.

Life rafts area on the back of the funnel aft.

View of the searchlights aft from port side.

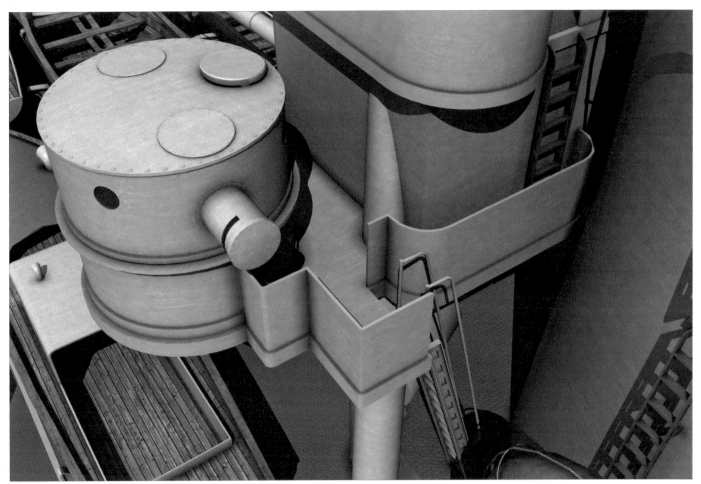

The rangefinder turret to control fire of the 100/47 mm turret aft from port side.

Views of the area with the supplied motor boats from port side.

View of the 100/47 mm anti-aircraft gun amidships from port side.

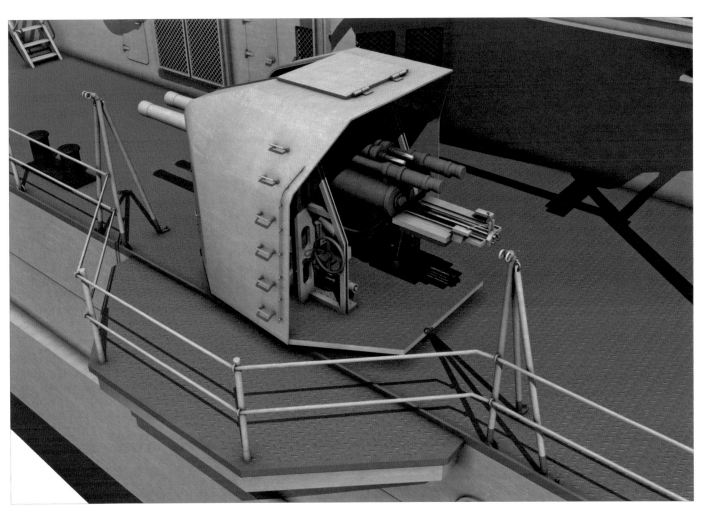

The Italian Heavy Cruiser Pola

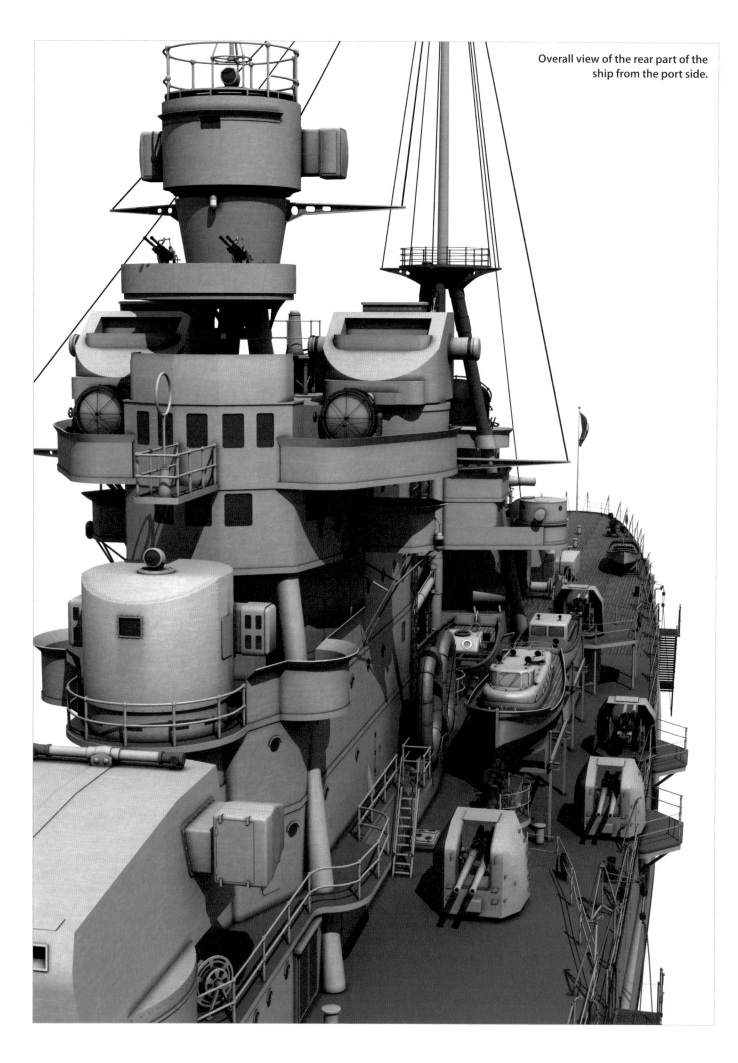

Overall view of the rear part of the ship from the port side.

The gangway at the bow from the port side.

Close-up view of the superstructure with the lookout platform and the red position lights.

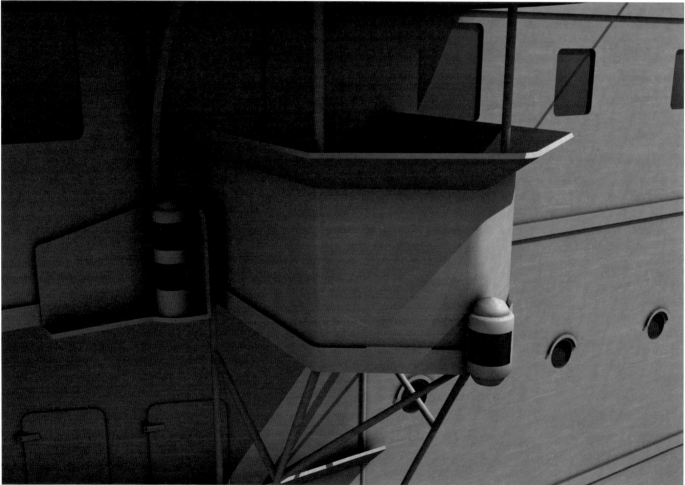

Overall view of the platform with two 13,2 mm anti-aircraft guns on top of the superstructure.

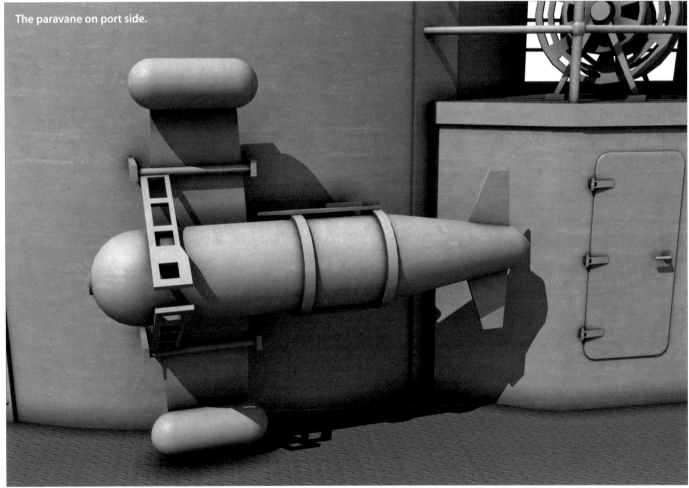

The paravane on port side.

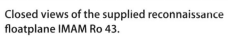

Closed views of the supplied reconnaissance
floatplane IMAM Ro 43.

The foredeck with the winches for the anchors.

The anchor on the port side.

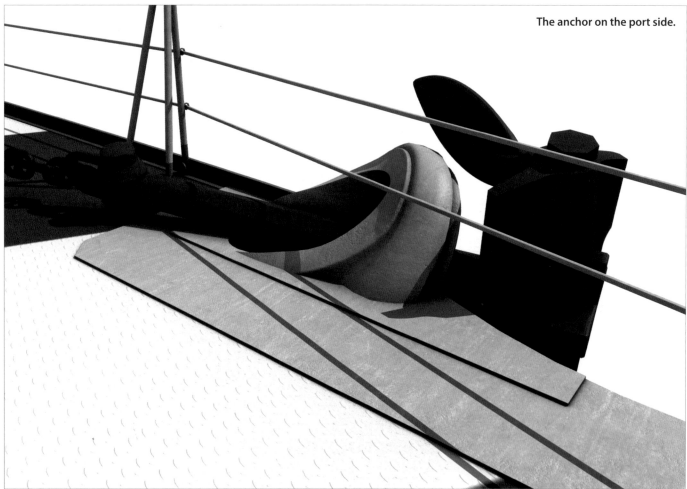

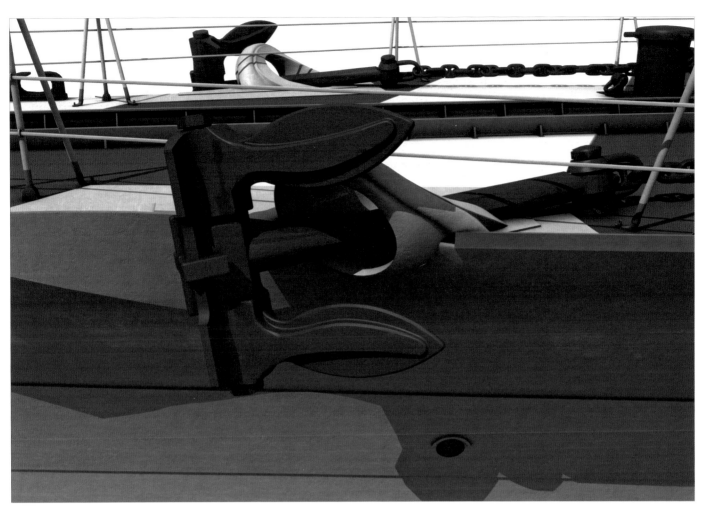

View of the bow.

Visit our shop online **shop.kagero.pl**

The Italian Heavy Cruiser Pola – Carlo Cestra
LUBLIN 2017 • ISBN 978-83-65437-46-4
© All rights reserved. With the exception of quoting brief passages for the purposes of review, no part of this publication may be reproduced without prior written permission from the Publisher.
3D illustrations and captions, text: **Carlo Cestra** • Proof-reading: **Tomasz Basarabowicz** • Design: **KAGERO STUDIO** – Marcin Wachowicz
KAGERO Publishing • www.kagero.pl, e-mail: kagero@kagero.pl, marketing@kagero.pl
Editorial office, Marketing, Distribution: KAGERO Publishing, Akacjowa 100, os. Borek, Turka, 20-258 Lublin 62, Poland, phone/fax (+48) 81 501 21 05
w w w . k a g e r o . e u